Where?

A DRAGON Question Book™

By Kathie Billingslea Smith
Illustrated by Robert S. Storms

A DRAGON BOOK

GRANADA

The stars do not go anywhere. Even in the daytime, the sky is full of stars, but we cannot see them because of the bright light of the sun. If we could block out the light from the sun, we would see the stars during the daytime, too.

during the day?

The stars are always there — morning, noon, and night. But sometimes, they cannot be seen because of the bright sunlight. When the sun sets at night, it is dark on our side of the earth. Then we can see the stars.

A flashlight's beam does not show up on a sunny day when there is plenty of light everywhere. But if you turn on that same flashlight at night when it is dark, the light will shine brightly.

Snow comes from clouds high up in the sky.

Clouds are made of tiny drops of water that have formed around bits of dust. When the air is cold enough, the drops of water freeze into tiny crystals of ice. These ice crystals join together to make snowflakes. When they become too heavy to

come from?

hang in the air, they fall down to the ground.

Then it snows! Millions and millions of snowflakes fall to the ground!

Sometimes when you are out in the snow, try to catch some snowflakes. Look at them carefully. Each snowflake has six sides. But no two snowflakes are alike. Each one has its own beautiful design.

The honeybee queen and some of her workers live through the winter inside their hive. In the fall, the workers collect sticky gum from trees. They use this to seal cracks in their beehive to make it safe and warm. Then when winter comes, they stay inside the hive.

When it grows cold, the bees crowd together to keep warm. They move their bodies and wings to make heat. They eat honey that they have stored in honeycombs during the summer.

go in winter?

Near winter's end, the queen bee begins laying eggs again. Soon the hive is busy with new worker bees making honey.

Air is the gas that covers the outside of the earth. You cannot see it, touch it, or taste it. But air is everywhere.

Air is inside rooms and cereal boxes and closets and pockets. Even when a room or box looks empty, air is still there.

Air is in caves and on top of mountains.

Air is even inside you! When you blow out the candles on your birthday cake, you are pushing air out of your body.

Or, when you blow up party balloons, that air is from inside you too.

People and plants need air to live. You breathe air in and out all day long.

The tallest building in the world is the Sears Tower in Chicago. It is 443 m high and has 110 floors! From the top,

you can see all over the city!

At 411 m, the World Trade Center in New York City, with its two towers, is only about 30 m

allest building?

shorter than the Sears Tower. This is about as tall as the famous Rock of Gibraltar found to the south of Spain. The third tallest building in the world is New York's Empire State Building, which soars 381 m above the bustling city.

Architects and engineers carefully designed all these buildings so that each would stand firm in bad storms and strong winds. Skyscrapers are also a great space-saving idea.

Think how much more land there is left to build on when buildings go up in the sky instead of spreading out all over the place!

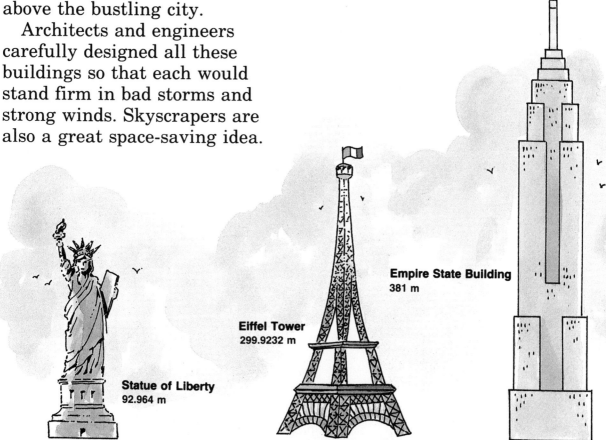

Statue of Liberty
92.964 m

Eiffel Tower
299.9232 m

Empire State Building
381 m

Chocolate grows on trees — but does not look like the sweets you like to eat!

Chocolate really comes from cacao beans. The beans are the seeds of the cacao fruit. They grow on cacao trees in lands where the weather is very hot.

The beans are dried and shipped to chocolate factories.

come from?

There they are roasted and ground up into cocoa butter. In a big mixer, the cocoa butter is blended with sugar and milk to make milk chocolate.

Then the chocolate is put in stores where we can buy it.

The next time you bite into a chocolate candy bar, think of the cacao trees where the story of chocolate begins!

Most paper is made from the wood of trees.

Lumberjacks cut down different kinds of trees and saw off the branches. Then the logs are loaded onto flatbed trucks and taken to a paper mill.

At the mill, the logs are cut up into little pieces. Then they are cooked and mixed with water to make pulp. The pulp is poured out onto big, flat screens to make wet paper. After the

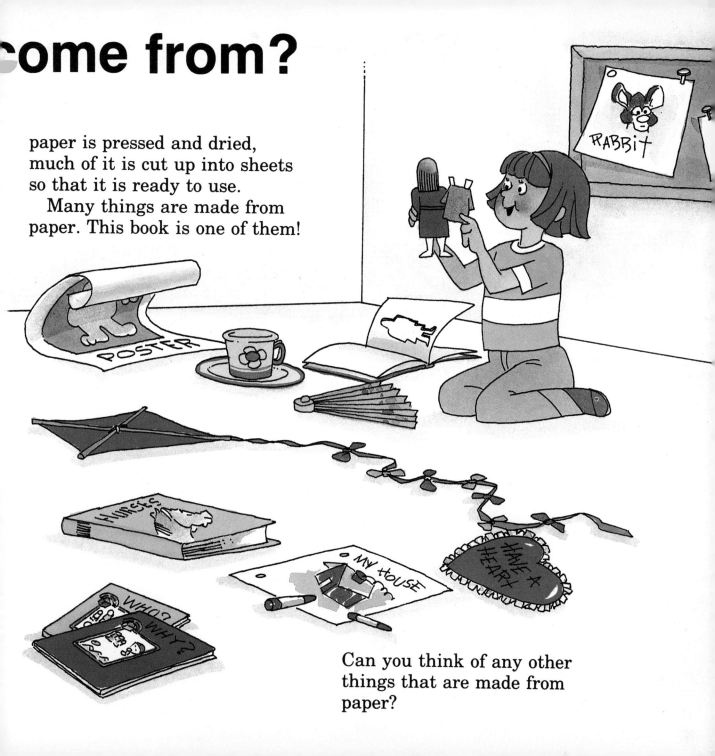

paper is pressed and dried, much of it is cut up into sheets so that it is ready to use.

Many things are made from paper. This book is one of them!

Can you think of any other things that are made from paper?

Astronauts will next build space stations and live in them in space, far away from Earth. The space stations will be supplied with all of the things that people need to live: air, food, water, and lights. Astronauts and other supplies will be flown from Earth to the space stations on space shuttles.

The astronauts will work and study in the space stations. They will use special cameras and laboratory equipment to learn more about space. Sometimes the astronauts will work outside the space stations.

astronauts go next?

Then they will wear space jet packs to help them move around in space. The astronauts will use special radios and televisions to talk with people back on Earth. When their missions are finished, the astronauts will fly back to Earth on the space shuttle.

Would you like to be an astronaut someday?

Where is the longest

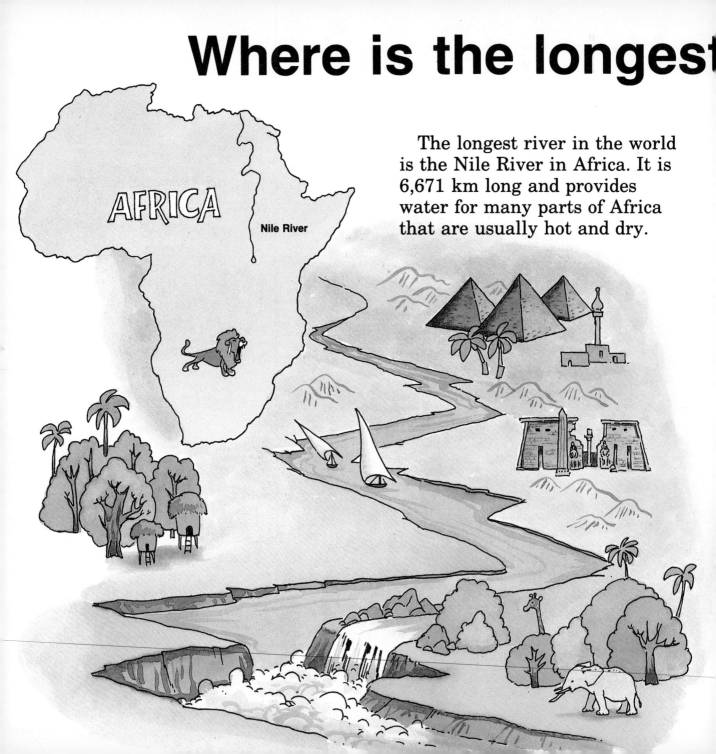

The longest river in the world is the Nile River in Africa. It is 6,671 km long and provides water for many parts of Africa that are usually hot and dry.

AFRICA

Nile River

iver in the world?

The Nile River starts in the center of Africa in a country called Burundi. Then it flows north and empties into the Mediterranean Sea by Egypt.

Many crocodiles swim in the Nile. As they work each day, farmers and fishermen living along the river banks must watch out for these creatures.

Dust is always in the air even when the air looks clear. If you shine a flashlight with a narrow beam in a dark room, you will see dust floating in the air. Sometimes dust settles on furniture in our houses. It looks like a fine, grey powder.

Dust is formed of tiny, dry pieces of earth or other objects that have crumbled or been worn away.

come from?

Dust from the soil is raised into the air every time a car drives down a road or a child runs across a yard.

Fireplaces spread ashes, and soot spews from chimneys.

Volcanoes give off explosions that turn hot liquid rock, called lava, into a spray of tiny drops and bits of glass. Volcanoes spread much of their dust across the earth.

Workshops add sawdust. Schoolrooms add chalkdust.

Some of the dust in the air even comes from outer space!

Where is the tallest

Of all the mountains on land, the tallest is Mount Everest. It is in the Himalaya Mountain Range on the border between the countries of Nepal and Tibet in Asia.

Mount Everest is 8,848 m tall. It soars high, high up toward the sky. Before it was named Mount Everest, it was called *Chomolungma*, which means "Mountain-So-High-No-Bird-Can-Fly-Over-It."

mountain in the world?

Mount Everest is covered with snow and ice. Blizzards and bad storms bring high winds and deep snows to the mountain.

Many people have tried to climb to the top of Mount Everest, but only a few have reached it safely. In 1953, Sir Edmund Hillary and Tenzing Norgay, a local villager, were the first people to climb to the top of the great mountain. Mountain climbers need ropes, mountain boots, ice axes, oxygen tanks, and light tents to travel up this peak.

Where do kangaroos live?

Far across the ocean is the land of Australia. Australia is both a country and a great continent. It is also an island with many strange and wonderful animals — many cannot be found in any other part of the world.

Kangaroos live on the grassy plains of Australia. With their strong back legs, kangaroos can leap farther than almost any other animal. Their long, heavy tails help them keep their balance when they hop. And kangaroos can leap as much as 7.5 metres in one jump!

Mother kangaroos carry their babies, or *joeys*, in their pouches.

There are many kinds of kangaroos. Tree kangaroos spend most of their time in trees. There are smaller kangaroos called wallabies. Others, only a foot long, are called rat kangaroos.

Some of Australia's other special animals are the koala bear, the platypus, and the anteater.